100 Ways to Save the World

Johan Tell

Edited by Kevin Billinghurst

BONNIER BOOKS

First Published by Bokförlaget Max Ström,
  Stockholm, Sweden 2007.
First published in the UK by Bonnier Books,
  Appledram Barns, Birdham Road, Chichester,
  West Sussex PO20 7EQ
©Bonnier Books, UK 2007
www.bonnierbooks.co.uk
Text: Johan Tell
Translation: Kevin Billinghurst
Graphic design: Patric Leo
Layout: Amelie Stenbeck-Ramel
All images from Johnér, www.johner.se
Printed by Fälth & Hässler, Värnamo, Sweden 2007
ISBN-13: 978-1-905825-40-0

Preface

The environment should be the dominant issue of our age. The threats to our natural world overshadow everything else, because they will determine the future for you and me and everything living on this planet. Protecting the environment is a basic issue of survival, and the good news is that that insight is sinking in among the politically and economically powerful circles where crucial decisions are made.

The global environmental situation is serious, but far from hopeless. Climate issues have risen to the top of the agenda in recent years, but in reality it's a larger matter of changing the short-sighted and irresponsible way we manage our common natural heritage: the atmosphere, the seas, fishing, farming, forestry, energy, transportation and all else that is affected by human activities.

But in spite of the obvious problems there are also enormous opportunities waiting to be addressed and huge profits to be won in the economic re-structuring that we must now undertake. Because without that new alignment of environmental and economic priorities, the coming century will indeed be a dire time.

This book is about the many things that we can do as individuals in our daily lives, and that makes it an important source of inspiration. Together with leading researchers, Johan Tell reveals a plethora of small steps we can take without great effort, expense or discomfort. Most of these suggestions are not only good for the environment; they're also good for your body, soul and family budget.

The first step toward a sustainable future is simply to gain insight and understanding. From there, the step toward engagement and action is not particularly large or difficult. When we succeed in changing our everyday habits we also make fundamental improvements in our very way of life, and that opens the door to the deeper political, economic and social change that must take place if we and our Earth are to survive together.

This book is one of the most stalwart and inspirational that I have ever read during my long career in the environmental movement. It gives hope and encourages action. I hope Johan Tell's book will be read by many, and that readers will be moved to use these simple, concrete tips.

Only together can we create our common future, and most of the work is still before us. But without the kind of inspiration contained in the book you hold in your hand, the public will never come to the realisation that the job is not to be left to experts. Every effort is important and no effort is too small.

Come along!

Professor Lars Kristoferson
Secretary General, WWF Sweden

It's time.

That became clear to me on the 17th of December 2006, when there were spring flowers blooming in my garden in Sweden where there should have been snow. I reached a tipping point on that winter day, a moment when I realized that I had to begin taking a new path. I had visited a glacier hotel with no glacier left, seen barren desert where there should have been vegetation, and carried my children through floods in Asia. But now it became clear. The time has come. Time to do something for our overstressed environment, for our common future.

The relationship between extreme weather conditions and the greenhouse effect is now widely accepted by the vast majority of mainstream scientists.

As far back as 1896, the Swedish chemist Svante Arrhenius became the first to speculate that changes in the levels of carbon dioxide in the atmosphere could substantially alter the Earth's surface temperature through what is now known as the greenhouse effect. More than a century later, the United Nations climate panel estimates that a doubling of atmospheric carbon dioxide levels will raise average temperatures by 4 degrees Celsius. Arrhenius figured it would take about 3,000 years, but then he could foresee neither the world's population explosion nor the massive increase in per capita energy consumption that was coming.

Perhaps Arrhenius's most important contribution was to show that the principle of the greenhouse effect - if we burn too much fossil fuel, temperatures will inevitably rise - is not so complicated that it couldn't be understood a hundred years ago.

Yet it took until 2006 for the UN climate panel to convince its most sceptical members to accept the scientific findings that key heat-trapping gases in the atmosphere "have increased markedly as a result of human activities", and that the evidence of the climate's warming "is unequivocal, as is now evident from observations of increases in global average air and ocean temperatures, widespread melting of snow and ice, and rising global mean sea level."

Still there are doubters who point out that natural phenomena such as volcanic eruptions or sunspots could explain temperature variations, and that the climate has always gone through changes and will continue to do so. Greenland is often cited to prove the point, since farming was possible there until about 1450. Or that a cold spell from 1590 to 1610 meant that Shakespeare's contemporaries could ice skate on the Thames every winter. Or that the Vikings' grape-growing Vinland has become today's pine-forested Newfoundland.

But there are precious few left who still doubt that humans also affect climate. Even the Bush administration admits that the greenhouse effect is a threat to species such as polar bears.

For the truth is that the American lifestyle, which is a looming disaster for the planet and which we Europeans imitate more and more, is too dependent on automobiles, junk food and disposable rubbish. The average American spends more time driving a car than on holiday. Why shouldn't such a lifestyle be negotiable?

Apart from strange weather, another event in 2006 helped bring the environmental debate to the front burner: release of the Stern Review, in which Sir Nicholas Stern presented a calculation of direct economic costs that we can expect to pay for climate change. The report estimates that global economic output will fall by at least 5 per cent and perhaps as much as 20 per cent unless strong measures are taken to reduce carbon emissions. Shifting to a low-carbon path could eventually benefit the economy by $2.5 trillion a year.

But the size of the Stern Review's price tag for climate change is perhaps less important than the simple fact that it is a price tag. Sir Nicholas, a well-tailored, well-educated, respected former chief economist at the World Bank, didn't scream out his message while chained to a tree and passing out pamphlets printed on recycled nappies. And his audience was not clad in hemp and podiatrically correct sandals, but included the world's leading economists, financiers and corporate leaders.

When environmental warnings begin to encompass the global economy, the market begins to listen. Suddenly there was a wider discussion of green capitalism, smart growth, and how companies can strive to be climate neutral by reducing carbon emissions and compensating for the rest by purchasing emission rights or planting trees.

Environmental issues leaked out of musty community centre meeting halls and into corporate boardrooms to the rustle of hastily assembled theme issues of Newsweek and The Economist.

Finally, it seemed that the environmental movement and the market were moving in the same direction.

Beyond the importance of bringing market forces to bear on climate change, the Stern Review highlighted the crucial role of politicians. The report was conducted under a mandate from the government, and Tony Blair called it "the most important document about the future I have read since becoming prime minister.

"There is little doubt that external factors led to Blair's ordering the report. To at least some extent, he chose to elevate environmental issues because they are important to the people of the nation.

That's why the most important thing you can do for the environment is not to switch to a green car or recycle your newspapers or buy low-energy lamps. The most effective way to make a difference is to make it clear to your politicians that you want to see environmental concerns addressed at the highest levels.

Democracy is not just a matter of going out to vote every few years when an election rolls around. Participating in democracy means maintaining a dialogue with those in power.

But while you communicate with elected officials, there are a lot of small choices you make that add up to big impacts – both direct effects like reduced energy consumption and waste, and indirectly by sending the right signals to politicians in your city, in parliament and in the European Union so they know they have the support they need to push for change.

Coming back from picking mushrooms in the woods I pass a barn. The cows inside are belching methane gas. A dairy herd can be seen as a symbol for our problems with greenhouse gases. It's not the gases themselves - in addition to carbon dioxide the Kyoto Protocol addresses methane, nitrous oxide, hydrofluorocarbons, perfluorocarbons, and sulphur hexafluoride - the problem is the amount of them. These gases are crucial to retaining the heat we need to live on Earth and to spreading out the heat we receive from the sun so that we have tolerable temperatures from the equator almost up to the poles. But an excess of greenhouse gases will cause temperatures to rise. Spring flowers bloom in December because we burn too much fossil fuel and have too many belching cows. It's that simple.

The Kyoto Protocol, which came into effect on February 16, 2006 and has been signed by 160 nations, calls for a 5 per cent reduction in greenhouse gases from 1990 figures by 2008-12.

If 5 per cent sounds like a small amount, it could be because 5 per cent is just that - too little. No serious observer believes that that reduction is enough to stop global warming.

We're going to have to make greater changes in our lives.

The first step is to recognize that we can't consume ourselves out of this crisis. Even if you always make the right environmental choices, buying more won't help. You'll have to learn to consume less. Get used to the idea that pretty much everything you use directly or indirectly contributes to carbon emissions: when you travel, when you eat and when you shop.

The greenhouse effect isn't the only environmental threat we face. My light outdoor jacket, designed to breathe out moisture while keeping body heat inside, is probably impregnated with substances that can cause liver damage and even cancer. The rot-resistant lumber I used to build a little pier contains chemicals that probably aren't good for marine life.

We seem to be surrounding ourselves with more and more

exotic chemicals and fewer and fewer exotic species.

Are there any positive signs? Of course there are.

• All EU countries, and as many more around the world, have developed strategies to replace fossil fuels with renewables.

• More and more politicians are putting environmental arguments on the agenda – even in the US.

• The global population is growing more slowly than earlier predictions suggested. A few years ago, the UN was predicting a 2050 population of more than 12 billion, but that figure has been reduced to 9 billion.

• The targets of the Kyoto Protocol may be modest, but signatures from 160 countries indicate that most of the world takes global warming seriously.

It's important to keep these positive signs in mind during a time when catastrophe warnings are constantly in the news. We all need to keep making the right small environmental decisions while we encourage politicians and corporate leaders to make the right big ones. Don't believe the pessimists who say it doesn't matter what we do as individuals. They're wrong. And don't forget what former US Vice President Al Gore said in his film "An Inconvenient Truth": "The danger is that people will go from denial to despair without stopping in between to ask themselves what action they can take."

It's time to recognise that we have to find new ways to think. If global warming is to be managed, we can no longer treat the planet's limited reserves of fossil fuel the way we have since the dawn of the industrial age. The oil and gas that is left in the ground needs to be conserved for higher-value uses than heating buildings and moving people and goods from one place to another. It's time to recognise that we need to make a leap beyond oil dependency. Or as Saudi Arabian Sheikh Zaki Yamani said: "The Stone Age didn't end for lack of stone, and the oil age will end long before the world runs out of oil."

Let's prove him right.

It's time.

1.

<u>CALL A POLITICIAN.</u> You can't change the world by yourself.
On the other hand, no politician can save the world without
you. Bringing change to environmental policies may require
regulation and prohibitions, or economic measures like
emissions trading. Either way, widespread popular support
is essential.

That's where your phone call comes in. Email is also a great
way to make yourself heard, and many politicians are on the
web, where other visitors may see your comments. Or why not
write a good, old-fashioned letter?

Even if you believe that the Earth can be saved only by
large, international political decisions, you can start by
getting in touch with local politicians. They interact with
parties and other politicians, and many are aiming for higher
office. You just might be talking to a future MP, and it's
not far from there to the European Parliament or the UN.

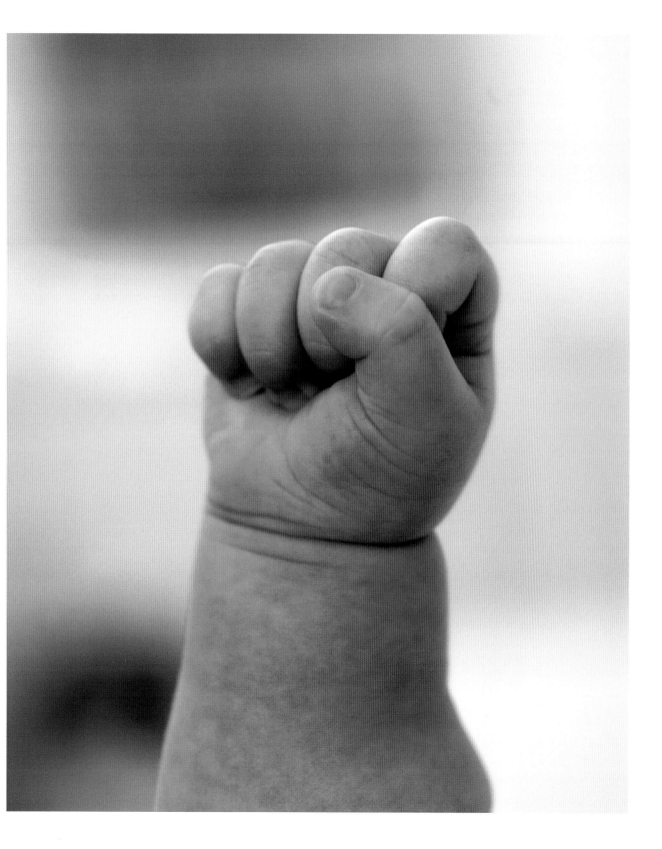

2.

BUY QUALITY. Shop for fewer, better products that will last longer. Enormous amounts of resources are wasted on poor-quality items that quickly get broken, wear out or simply go out of fashion. A good pair of shoes should last ten years, a car twenty, a piece of furniture two — generations, that is.

  Don't buy things that won't last. Don't buy things you'll get tired of. Only throw things away when they're worn out. You might have to pay more, but you'll pay a lot less often.

3.

SINK THOSE PIRATES. When you buy unauthorized copies of name-brand goods, there's a good risk you'll be buying a product made by underage workers in sweatshop factories.

  You may or may not think designer labels are worth the extra money, but global companies at least face a certain amount of pressure to maintain their images and not be exposed as villains. Most big companies publish ethics codes, and they have to respect minimum wage laws, environmental controls and negotiated working conditions. Pirates can't be held responsible for anything.

4.

UNDERSTAND WHAT YOU BUY. If the content label on a product lists mostly compounds that you're not familiar with, there's a good chance that they aren't the best things for your body or for the ecosystem.

5.

TAKE THE TRAIN. Rail travel is a clear environmental winner over aeroplanes and cars. Some estimates put carbon dioxide releases from air travel at ten times as much per passenger mile as a train. Others say it's three hundred times as much. It all depends on the distance travelled, since aeroplanes pollute most on take-off and landing. Of course, there's also a big difference depending on whether the train runs on electricity from renewable sources or from fossil fuel.

Also, the train is also simply a more civilized way to travel. You can meet people, sleep, work or enjoy a drink.

6.

CONNECT THE DOTS. It's not a wild exaggeration to say that everything contributes to global warming. Pretty much all production releases carbon dioxide, as does all motorised transportation. And that's especially true of all those gadgets that run on electricity, whether from the mains or from batteries, as well as anything powered by petrol, diesel, gas or ethanol.

You don't need to learn how everything works. But a basic understanding of how different products are connected to energy consumption will help you figure out where you can save. To put it into context, let's say you'd like to cut your personal carbon output by 250 kg. You could:

• Replace nine 60-Watt standard light bulbs with low energy compact fluorescent lights. During the life of these long-lasting lamps you'll save 250 kg of carbon.

• Replace 1,200 kilometres of car travel with bicycling.

• Cut your driving speed from 110 kph to 90 kph for 6000 kilometres.

• Replace a two-stroke outboard boat motor with a four-stroke. In just 30 hours of running time you'll save 250 kg of carbon.

• Replace the meat in one of every four dinners with legumes. A family of four will save 250 kg of carbon in a year.

If none of these suggestions is quite right, you can plant 21 trees. Your trees will absorb about 250 kg of carbon a year, and they should keep working for at least another forty years or so.

To get a clear picture of how lifestyle choices contribute to the greenhouse effect, check out the European Commission's Carbon Calculator.

7.

SEE NATIVE WILDLIFE. Ecotourism doesn't have to mean travelling abroad. Environmentally themed destinations abound throughout Britain. Take a boat trip to the waters around the Hebrides and see huge minke whales or playful harbour porpoises and dolphins. Or go bird watching in Wales or biking in Devon where you might see deer, foxes, badgers and otters. Visit one of our 14 national parks.

Take a weekend trip by bus or train and simply check into a hostel, go paddling in a lake or take a hike along the coast and see where you wind up.

8.

EAT NATIVE WILDLIFE. Consumption of game meats is growing fast in Britain, and that's mostly a good thing for the environment. Sales of game — including venison (deer), rabbit, pheasant, partridge and wild boar — went up 46 per cent between 2004 and 2006. The days are gone when those meats were associated solely with the gentry and poachers; you can now easily find venison and game birds for sale in butchers' shops and well-stocked supermarkets.

About five times as much energy is required to bring a kilo of beef to your local shop as a kilo of venison. As a bonus, game is generally lower in fat and cholesterol than beef and pork, and more flavourful than chicken. Venison accounts for the largest share of the game market, and is sold in burgers, sausages and steaks. Free-range and organic deer populations need regular culling because their predators are long gone. The meat offers a tasty, healthful alternative to factory-farmed meats.

9.

SWITCH ELECTRIC COMPANIES. British electrical power is largely generated by fossil fuels — coal, oil and natural gas. If we are to substantially reduce our emissions of greenhouse gases, this will need to change. By switching to green electricity, you send a positive market signal to producers.

Choose an electricity provider offering renewable energy from wind, solar, hydro or tidal power.

10.

<u>USE YOUR HANDS.</u> Look for ways to be your own power source. The physical effort won't hurt, and you can cut down on some of those unnecessary electric gadgets. Remember, carbon is released in manufacturing, transportation to the store, and generating electricity.

Just because somebody came up with the idea of selling a battery-powered, self-lighting pepper mill doesn't mean you need one. The same goes for electric corkscrews. You can whip cream, brush your teeth and make foamy milk for your cappuccino manually. Stronger wrists just might help your tennis game.

11.

<u>BE A GREEN SPORT.</u> Almost everybody needs to get more exercise. Why not go for a jog or a bicycle ride right from your front door instead of taking the car to a gym? Football consumes less energy than Formula 1 racing. And isn't "motor sports" an oxymoron anyway? Maybe it's time to ask if motor car and motorcycle racing make sense in a warming world.

12.

EAT FROM THE SEA. Fish, mussels, crab and other seafood are excellent sources of high-value protein. Enjoy the bounty of the sea. But give it some thought, too, because a good many environmental problems are connected to fish and shellfish.

Industrialised fishing is a threat to many species, so take it easy on cod, tuna, shark and halibut. If you're unsure which fish are sustainably managed, take the Marine Stewardship Council's handy pocket-sized guide to fish along to the shops.

Some fish are known to concentrate environmental poisons such as mercury and pesticides. That's why nutritionists now recommend eating only one serving a week of fish from the beleaguered Baltic Sea. Which fish is right for you from an environmental point of view depends to a large extent on where you live. Talk to your local fishmonger and find out what he or she thinks is the best local choice. See if your local shop offers eco-labelled fish.

With its rich maritime traditions and proximity to North Sea fisheries, Britain is blessed with excellent choice in seafood. So do we really need to eat fish sticks from whitefish caught far out in the Atlantic — or even the northern Pacific — frozen at sea, shipped to China, thawed, processed, re-frozen and shipped to Europe? Probably not.

13.

PLAY IT AGAIN, SAM: RECYCLE. Mixed refuse is a gigantic environmental problem as well as an economic cost paid through your taxes. Separated rubbish, on the other hand, is an economic resource.

Recycling an aluminium container saves 95 per cent of the energy required to make a new one. An 11-Watt low-energy lamp can run for 33 hours on the energy saved by recycling a single plastic PET bottle. A tonne of recycled paper saves 17 trees (we need those trees to process our excess carbon).

So get in the habit of sorting plastic, metal, glass, paper and batteries. Old paint, chemicals, oil, electronics and appliances should be taken to the recycling centre for proper disposal.

14.

BUY LARGER QUANTITIES. Packaging waste accounts for fully one-quarter of everything that goes in the bin, and most of that can be recycled. But even better from the perspective of resources and energy is to avoid bringing excess packaging home from the store in the first place. Look for refillable containers whenever you shop. If you can't find them ask to talk to the store manager.

15.

DON'T TOSS BATTERIES. Battery recycling is a relatively new field for the UK. While we recycle more than 90 per cent of our lead acid batteries — those used in vehicles — just 4 per cent of the non-lead acid waste batteries produced each year in the UK are recycled.

This means that, of about 25,000 tonnes of waste household and industrial batteries generated in the UK each year, just 1,000 tonnes are recycled. Deposited in a landfill, batteries can leak cadmium, mercury and lead into the environment.

Other European countries have more impressive recycling rates and their own battery re-processing facilities, often subsidised by the state. In the UK, some councils are beginning to offer battery recycling services, mostly at the request of residents. Check and see if your local recycling centre takes batteries or is planning to start.

16.

KEEP YOUR GARDEN GREEN. If we can't apply environmental principles around our own homes, how we can expect farmers to think ecologically?

Do you really need pesticides and herbicides? Look at what you have in the garden shed and see if there's a better alternative. We use more chemicals per square metre in our gardens than is used in forestry and fruit orchards.

Have a look at your machines. Do you really need all these noisemakers? Is it possible to take care of your garden with hand tools?

If you need a power mower, choose an electric model. If that isn't practical, a four-stroke emits less pollution and runs quieter than a two-stroke. Always use green fuel; that can cut your carbon output by up to 90 per cent.

Irrigate with rainwater, and time your watering for sunset, when you won't lose so much to evaporation. Try to use a hose rather than sprinklers; otherwise you may waste everything you've saved with low-flow toilets and showers.

Try just changing your attitude. One person's overgrown garden is another person's haven for butterflies, birds, hedgehogs and other wildlife. Try to save a patch of nettles in your garden. You don't have to go near them, but butterflies love them. The mother butterfly lays her eggs on the underside of the nettle leaf, and when the caterpillar emerges the leaf provides essential nutrition. Those caterpillars will attract beautiful birds into your garden.

A hammock is just about the most environmentally sound addition imaginable for your garden.

Think about what's important in your garden. Do you want a neat and tidy show garden, full of non-native plant species, or do you prefer a patch of wild nature? Beauty, after all, is in the eye of the beholder.

17.

GIVE LIVING PLANTS. British consumers spend more than a billion pounds every year on cut flowers, and about one-third of that is for imports. But it's not hard to find ways to cheer up our homes with floral colour and scent and still avoid pesticides, artificial fertilizers and air transportation. Next time you visit your local florist, look first at the potted plants. Your dinner host will be just as happy, and the gift will last much longer. Season permitting, you might even put out a little extra effort and make your own bouquet of local wildflowers.

Be careful not to trespass when picking flowers and never take them from a nature reserve or protected site without permission. Untended road verges and public rights of way are often good sources of wildflowers.

18.

THINK ABOUT YOUR DRINK. After acquiring a reputation for inferiority some years ago, ecologically produced wines and beers have made dramatic improvements. Vineyards in warm climates have done the best job of cutting out chemical pesticides, probably because the fungi that attack grapes prefer damp environments. A Google search on "organic wine" will get hundreds of hits from producers all over the world. Also on the web, the consumer guide About Organics provides information and links to organic suppliers across the UK, including makers of wine, beer, lager and cider.

19.

<u>DEMAND BETTER TRAIN CONNECTIONS.</u> Too few of us travel to the Continent by train. And no wonder: the best rail ticket from London to Milan requires sixteen hours and four connections, and it costs ten times as much as a low-price air ticket. A direct high-speed train could make the trip in under three hours.

Send an email to your MEP and ask why we don't have better train connections to Europe.

20.

SWITCH TO A GREEN CAR. Road transport accounts for about one-fourth of Britain's total carbon emissions, and switching to a green car is probably the best way for a private person to drastically reduce contributions to greenhouse gases.

Biogas is the best environmental fuel choice available today. Produced from sewage sludge, pharmaceutical waste or separated household rubbish, biogas causes no net increase in greenhouse gases.

It's easier to find petrol stations offering LPG, which, while a fossil fuel and hence not a renewable energy source, is nonetheless a better choice than petroleum fuels since it produces about 25 per cent lower greenhouse gas emissions.

Bioethanol, a blend of ethanol and petrol, is environmentally inferior to biogas, but is far more practical for most motorists because automobiles built to run on bioethanol can also be fuelled with petrol. The net carbon contribution from bioethanol cars is 60 to 80 per cent lower than from petrol engines.

Hybrid electric vehicles combine batteries and a conventional petrol engine under the bonnet (bioethanol hybrids are in development). Hybrids are best at low speeds and stop-and-start driving — for instance delivery rounds — when the car runs on batteries. Electric hybrids save an estimated 25 to 40 per cent of the fuel used by a conventional vehicle.

Green vehicles can also include extremely efficient cars with petrol engines getting more than 60 miles per gallon.

21.

PLEASE (DON'T) STANDBY. Some of your appliances use up to half as much energy on standby as they do when they're in use. If you turn off your TV, clock radio, computer and broadband connection when they aren't being used, you can save money and cut down on your contribution to global warming.

A plug-in electric meter helps you find out which appliances in your home are consuming the most energy, and can help you decide whether they should be turned off.

22.

SWITCH IT OFF. The folk musician Arlo Guthrie once said, "You can't have a light without a dark to stick it in." So let empty rooms be dark rooms. And switching to modern low energy bulbs will save money as well as reducing your "carbon footprint". The new compact fluorescent bulbs cost more to buy, but they last about ten times longer than incandescents. If you use a lamp four to five hours a day, a low energy bulb will pay for itself in less than a year. Switching from a 60 Watt incandescent bulb to an 11 Watt fluorescent puts the same amount of light into the room, and it cuts your carbon output by about 58 kilos per year.

23.

WASH SMART. Avoid pre-washing and fabric softener. Don't use more detergent than necessary. Always wash with a full load, and use lower temperatures when possible. Washing at 40 degrees consumes about half as much energy as 60 degrees, and there's seldom any need to wash at 90 degrees. Low-pollution washing powder gets your clothes just as clean.

24.

DISH IT OUT. One household appliance that can actually cut your energy consumption while making life a lot easier is the dishwasher. But only if you make sure the machine is full before turning it on, use the Economy program and turn off the auto-dry function. If your dishwasher has its own heating element (most do these days), connect the incoming line to cold water so you won't be rinsing in hot.

25.

SAVE WATER. Even before you heat it up, water consumes energy when it's purified and pumped to your house. Don't let the tap run more than necessary, and if it's dripping get it fixed. Check into low-flow toilets. If you're not in a position to replace your old full flush toilet, Thames Water will send you a free device called a hippo that saves up to three litres of water with every flush. You can have a free hippo even if you are not in the Thames Water area.

26.

DRINK ORGANIC COFFEE. Not just for the sake of your own well-being, but also because pesticides are an enormous threat to the health of people in coffee-growing regions. In Costa Rica alone, about 700 people fall acutely ill every year, and 30 die, from toxic chemicals that were banned long ago in Europe.

Organic coffee plantations also follow more long-term, sustainable strategies for preserving biodiversity. In Britain, only about one cup of coffee in 25 is from organic beans. That's too little.

Fairtrade certification requires coffee growers to adhere to basic environmental management principles, as well as guaranteeing that small farmers receive fair prices for their crops, that workers are allowed to organise, and that a share of profits from coffee farming are directed toward community development.

Fairtrade also certifies tea, cocoa, cotton and much more. Not all Fairtrade certified products are organic, but it's worth looking for the Fairtrade Mark in your supermarket. If you don't see it, ask your grocer why.

27.

LOVE YOUR SEWER. Let's admit it, most of us don't get all warm and fuzzy over the contents of our sewers. But they're not improved by adding paints, heavy metals, oils, solvents or chemicals. If it weren't for the pollutants, we would be able to use sewage sludge to fertilise fields for growing crops.

The toilet is no place to dispose of anything that it's not designed for, including cotton, cigarette butts, condoms, plasters, razor blades, tampons or letters from the girl who broke your heart. All that flotsam and jetsam just makes the sewage treatment plant work harder.

28.

MAKE YOUR OWN EARTH. It only takes a small outdoor space to set up your own compost bin, and taking the food waste out of your rubbish bin can cut by half the amount that has to be transported to a landfill. At the same time, you'll be making perfect soil for your potted plants or vegetable garden. If you don't have an outdoor space, think about investing in a wormery. This is a self-contained box into which you put your food waste and in return get a rich organic compost. Don't worry, the worms entertain themselves and they can't get out.

29.

ATONE. You can compensate for your excess contribution to carbon dioxide releases. Here are three simple ways, though there are many more:

• Buy offsets to cover the carbon released when you travel by air on holiday. That environmental debt will then be paid by, for instance, an electricity generator or a shipping company. See www.carbon-clear.com.

• Plant trees to absorb carbon. As an example, if you fly round-trip from London to Milan, you can support a project to plant 30 trees. In one year, your debt will be cleared. Schemes for compensating carbon dioxide releases from air travel by sponsoring tree planting projects are offered by Green Seats (www.greenseat.com) and Climate Care (www.climatecare.org)

• Support projects aiming to replace fossil fuels with renewables. That can be anything from windmill electric generators to subsidies for solar ovens in the developing world.

30.

LEARN ABOUT THE WATER FRAMEWORK DIRECTIVE. Major sources of water pollution from mining, sewage and industry have improved tremendously in recent decades. But there are still thousands of "diffuse" polluters threatening the fish we eat, the water we drink and the health of our lakes and rivers. That may be about to change.

The EU Water Framework Directive (WFD), passed in 2000, is the most substantial piece of water legislation ever adopted in Europe. It requires all inland and coastal waters to reach "good status" by 2015 — though there are already doubts as to whether that target is realistic. Even if it falls short of the high hopes held by its framers, the directive promises a huge leap forward in management of water resources across Europe by structuring decisions more according to the geography of river basins and less based on the political boundaries of nations, counties and cities.

This "integrated catchment management" aims to maximize synergies and minimize conflicts.

If it's properly implemented by the EU member states (and that's a big if) WFD could emerge as the poster child for European co-operation on environmental issues.

An important feature of the directive is that it encourages active public involvement in the decision-making process about future investments in pollution control. An intensive period of public consultation, continuing until the end of 2009, will set priorities, draft river basin management plans, and develop programmes to meet environmental targets.

Powerful economic interests can be expected to make their views known during this process. People whose sole agenda is a healthy water environment for generations to come should be at the table too.

31.

LEAVE THE MUSKY SCENT TO OXEN. Natural musk, a glandular extract from musk oxen, beavers and musk deer, has long been used in medicine and as a scent enhancer in perfumes.

As the price of natural musk has skyrocketed in recent decades, the cosmetics industry has almost completely converted to synthetic compounds containing muscone, the active ingredient. The same chemicals are widely used in soaps, detergents and fabric softeners, leading to increased levels in aquatic environments. While the health impacts of synthetic musk are not yet confirmed, there is concern that it affects oestrogen production, and may be bad for humans as well as fish.

32.

AVOID BROMINATED FLAME RETARDANTS. These compounds are linked to behavioural, learning and reproductive disturbances. Like the infamous and now-banned PCBs and DDT, brominated flame retardants are easily absorbed by organisms of all kinds and very slow to break down in the environment.

When you're shopping, ask if products contain brominated flame retardants. You may be told that these chemicals are present, but that they pose no risk to the user of a dishwasher, or a sofa, or a computer. That may or may not be true, but it's a bad answer in any case. At some point in the future, those products must be disposed of, and there is no guarantee that they'll be treated as hazardous waste.

The EU has prohibited two of these compounds, PBB and PBDE. Encourage your MEP to support restrictions on the remaining 70 or more variants.

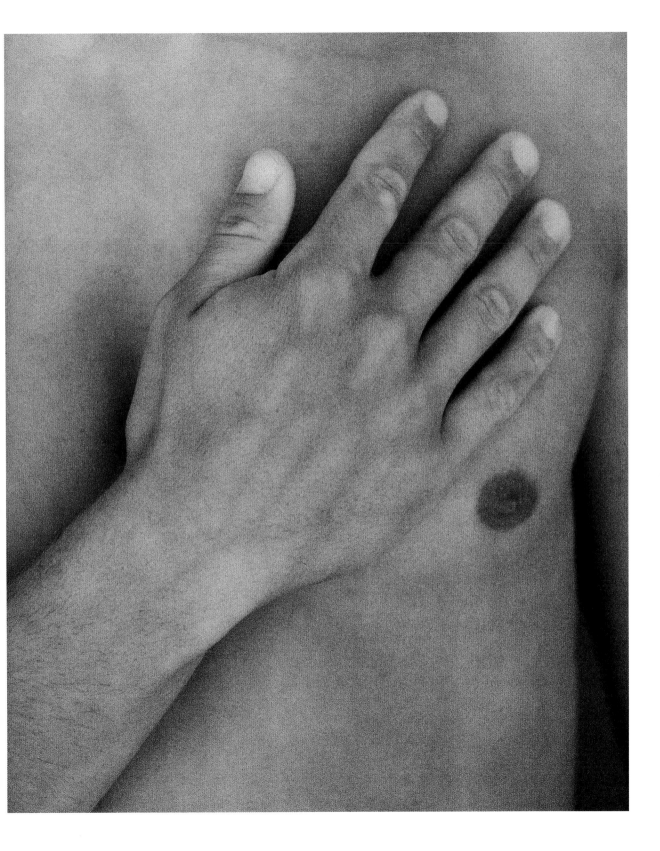

33.

LET THE MERCURY FALL. Energy consumption drops by up to 5 per cent if you lower the thermostat by just 1°C. In the average single-family home, going from 22° to a still-comfortable 20° will reduce carbon dioxide production by 140 tons per year and save up to £80. Wear a pair of slippers and maybe a jumper and you'll never even notice the difference.

34.

DON'T LET THE MERCURY OUT. Mercury is a highly toxic environmental pollutant that can cause severe brain damage, especially in children. As an element, it cannot be broken down by natural processes.

The EU Commission has proposed eliminating mercury from measurement tools, where an estimated 33 tonnes are used each year.

Most batteries are mercury-free these days, though many button batteries used in cameras, watches, hearing aids and other small apparatuses still contain mercury. Make sure these are disposed of properly, and watch out for things like thermometers, circuit-breakers and electrical switches.

35.

PROTECT YOUR CHILDREN. A large study of creams, oils and
shampoos gave a thumbs-down to more than 70 per cent. Of 69
products tested, 50 contained chemicals deemed hazardous to
children's health, the environment, or both. A few basic rules:
• Avoid perfumes and dyes
• Use baby oil instead of soap for infants
• Don't buy disposable wet wipes. Instead, if you're going out
with small kids, just carry along a wet flannel with a little
gentle soap in a plastic bag.
• Yes, cloth nappies are still best, for your baby, for the
environment and for your budget. You can save several hundred
pounds during those first three years, and even more if you
have another child.

36.

BE ANTI-ANTIBACTERIAL. Not all bacteria are bad, and it's
possible to make your home "too clean". We've always lived with
bacteria all around us, and your child's immune system needs
to be stimulated by some exposure to bacteria in order to be
healthy enough to defend against those really aggressive ones
that might make her sick.
    When the label brags that a product kills 99.9 per cent
of bacteria, think about that .01 per cent. They survive and
reproduce, and they're turning into resistant strains that are
causing new environmental hazards. Antibacterial agents are
being added to everything from toothpaste and dishcloths to
socks and sports clothing. One company has even released a line
of antibacterial pencils. Have you ever seen a sick pencil?
    It's unnecessary. If you're not performing surgery, good
old-fashioned hygiene and simple soaps do just fine.

37.

KEEP ON ROLLIN'. The right pressure in your tyres reduces fuel consumption — enough to save you £50 per year while cutting carbon dioxide by 140 tonnes.

Next time you have to buy new, look for green tyres. The ordinary models in use on most cars contain cancer-causing oils that wind up in the environment as the tyre wears down. These oils are banned in the EU from January 2010, but you don't have to wait until then to do your part.

38.

STICK TO THE SPEED LIMIT. Fuel consumption — and accompanying greenhouse gas emissions — increases by about 30 per cent as your speed goes from 50 to 70 miles per hour. And then it increases by 60 percent when you go from 70 to 90 mph. Lower driving speeds also save lives.

39.

EAT WITH THE SEASON. Local, seasonal food requires less energy to grow and transport. It's generally less expensive than food that is scarcer or has travelled a long way and it tends to be fresher, tastier and more nutritious.

Brussels sprouts, cauliflower, apples and pears are great winter food. Asparagus, peas, cherries and strawberries are at their best in the summer.

40.

EAT YOUR VEGETABLES. Your mother was right, but perhaps not for the same reasons we're talking about here. One kilo of beef is equivalent to seven litres of petroleum. Eating lower down on the food chain requires less energy. It's better for the planet if you eat soybeans rather than animals raised on soybeans. It's not necessary to become a vegetarian, but you might try leaving the meat out of one dinner each week.

In addition to energy use, livestock farming causes other problems. One is the destruction of rainforests to make space for grazing land, which reduces biodiversity and kills off big, carbon-absorbing trees. Another is the amount of methane produced by cattle, goats and sheep. Methane is a powerful greenhouse gas — its effect is up to 25 times as damaging as carbon dioxide. The animals we eat produce more greenhouse gases than the entire transportation sector — an incredible 18 per cent of the worldwide total.

From an environmental perspective, chicken is a better alternative than red meat for animal protein.

41.

PLAN YOUR SHOPPING. Try to avoid unnecessary trips to the
store in your car. On average, the food we eat has travelled
50 per cent further than it did just 20 years ago. Much of this
is due to increased imports of food — and there's no denying
that variety, freshness and quality are improved by transport
networks. But half of the total carbon dioxide load generated
by food — from farm to table — comes at the consumer end,
mainly in getting it home from the store.

There's a big difference in environmental impact between
transporting food in fully loaded lorries and carrying a couple
bags in the boot of your car.

42.

COMMUTE SMART. Private car travel accounts for about half
of all carbon dioxide emissions from the transportation sector,
and daily commuting to jobs and school generates most of that.
That's a good place to start looking for ways to conserve
energy.

Public transportation is far better. Ride a bike or walk if
you can. A 25-kilometre round-trip commute to work each day
amounts to approximately 7,400 kilometres per year. That's the
carbon dioxide equivalent of 1.8 tonnes, the same amount you
would generate by flying to Thailand on holiday.

43.

PLANT TREES. By making a contribution to a tree-planting project, you can help restore a rainforest or stop desert sands from claiming more productive land. All the growing plants in Europe absorb barely 10 per cent of the carbon we generate, which means we Europeans have an enormous "tree debt" to the rest of the world.

By planting trees, you're shaping a better future.

44.

REFUSE DIRECT ADVERTISING. A huge amount of trees, ink and energy are wasted in printing and distributing direct-mail advertising that goes straight from the mailbox to the bin. If you read the ads, great. If you don't, put up a "No junk mail, please" sign. That will be about 50 kilos a year that you don't have to carry out for recycling.

45.

BE ECO-CHIC. It's time to take a fresh look at the term ecological, which, let's face it, has acquired a ring of self-righteous finger-wagging. Ecological thinking is no longer a list of don'ts seemingly aimed at making life boring. Looking at your personal impact on the web of life can open doors to fulfilling experiences and meaningful change.

You don't have to live in a commune and eat lentil soup at every meal. Ecology has actually become chic, even trendy, and fuel for some great cocktail-party chatter. Check out eco-resorts, eco-sports, eco-holidays, eco-pets, eco-homes, eco-design, eco-furniture, eco-art and eco-weddings.

46.

AVOID PLASTIC. To be sure, plastic is the only choice for many uses. It's light, strong, flexible, waterproof and inexpensive. But many plastics are associated with chemical pollution, both in manufacturing and in final disposal. PVC plastics are among the worst offenders, because they usually contain softeners (called ftalates) which have been shown to cause cancer, disrupt hormone function and affect the liver and reproductive organs. PVC products are marked with a triangle and the number 3. They're found in a wide range of products and packaging materials.

Plastics are manufactured mainly from petroleum and natural gas, and that means they contribute to the greenhouse effect.

Where possible, buy environmentally sound goods made from glass, leather, wood, cotton or wool. They feel nicer, last longer and age better.

47.

ENJOY A BARBECUE. But avoid lighting the charcoal with toxic
petroleum distillates. Instead, use a chimney starter — an up-
right metal tube with a heatproof handle and a wire partition
in the centre. Just put a few sheets of newspaper in the bottom
and the briquettes in the top, and light the paper with a
match.

Charcoal isn't really the best use of timber — one hectare
of forest could produce 150,000 kilogrammes of timber but just
one-tenth of that in charcoal. Fortunately, it doesn't take a
great deal of charcoal to feed your barbecue. But most of the
charcoal sold in the UK comes from tropical woods, which means
it contributes to deforestation of tropical habitats.

Fossil fuel grills contribute to global warming (charcoal is
carbon neutral), but they also burn cleaner. Gas is preferable
to electricity.

48.

SIT PRETTY. Choose outdoor furniture made from wood or cast
iron rather than plastic. Look for products made from European
pine, alder or oak instead of buying tropical woods that
have been transported halfway round the world. If you do buy
tropical woods, make sure your tables and benches come with
an eco-label. It's no guarantee, but certainly reduces the
likelihood that you'll be contributing to the destruction of
rainforests.

49.

DRINK TAP WATER. Anywhere you go in Britain, water from the tap is perfectly safe to drink. Building factories to bottle water, load it onto lorries and drive it out to stores is a waste of energy and resources.

There's little reason for concern over water quality. In 2003, Britain's Drinking Water Inspectorate carried out some 2.9 million tests on drinking water samples in England and Wales, of which 99.88 per cent passed.

Still, consumption of bottled water is approaching 2 billion litres per year, and growing steadily. It appears that much of that represents people drinking bottled water as an alternative to sugary fizzy drinks, which is probably a good thing for public health. But if your tap water is just as good, why pay a thousand times as much for water that contributes to global warming?

50.

SAVE IN THE KITCHEN. When it's time to replace your fridge, freezer, stove or dishwasher, look for the most energy-efficient models. All white goods are labelled for energy consumption, and you should be looking for A to A+++ ratings. A new refrigerator and freezer can save as much as £50 per year and cut out a few kilos of carbon dioxide emissions.

But there's no need to switch before your current machines are at the end of their useful life. A lot of resources and energy go into making appliances.

While you're waiting, make sure you regularly vacuum the coils on the back of the fridge so the compressor won't need to work as hard to maintain a low temperature. De-frosting also cuts the load on the compressor, as does letting warm food cool to room temperature before putting it in to chill.

51.

CONTACT A COMPANY. Take the time to call or email a consumer panel. Ask questions about contents, manufacturing practices, packaging and transportation.

Companies are very careful to track these statistics, and nothing is more effective at changing corporate behaviour than consumer pressure.

52.

ASK QUESTIONS. Do you own stocks? Use your right to get answers from management at annual shareholder meetings. Be concrete: Has the company looked into hybrids for its car fleet or delivery vehicles? Is there a plan to balance carbon emissions? Has the company achieved ISO 14001 environmental certification?

Management is obliged to answer these questions, and to make their replies available for shareholders who don't attend the meeting, usually by posting questions and answers on the corporate website.

53.

SUPPORT RESPONSIBLE COMPANIES. Most large European companies — and many small and mid-sized enterprises — publish reports on their efforts to limit environmental impacts. These reports may be anything from a brief statement on a website to thorough documentation printed and distributed to shareholders along with the company annual report.

54.

USE THE INTERNET. Download music. Legal downloads are less expensive than CDs. Less energy and resources are consumed by downloading than by pressing and distributing physical CDs.

The same goes for newspapers, magazines, catalogues and audiobooks. Even films, if you have a newish computer and a broadband connection.

But a good book should still be read on paper. For the time being at least, no computer monitor can substitute.

55.

USE THE LIBRARY. Borrowing books, CDs and films is a resource-saving form of cultural recycling.

agmente
über
mation.
Zur
nterung
des
und vierten Bandes
des
u m s.
Von
Rambach,
es Heft.
nd Stettin,

56.

<u>CHECK YOUR CHEMICALS.</u> Go through the products you use in the kitchen, bathroom and laundry. Read the content labels, find out if they're harmful to the environment and make a decision on whether you really need them in your home.

57.

<u>THINK GLOBALLY, ACT LOCALLY (WITHIN REASON).</u> If we were to blindly follow this simplistic bumper sticker sentiment in our eating habits, we'd have to go back to living half the year on salt beef and turnips.

All else being equal, however, local food bought in season is a better choice than exotic foods shipped — or worse, flown — into Britain.

Hundreds of different varieties of apples are grown in England, Scotland, Wales and Ireland. Look in the store for Bramley or Cox', or perhaps Discovery, Worcester or Egremont Russet, before picking out a green apple from Argentina. British early potatoes may take a few weeks longer to reach your store's shelves than the ones flown in from the Canary Islands, but they're worth the wait.

That doesn't mean that food produced in Britain is always the best environmental choice. An imported sun-ripened tomato may require less energy than one grown in a hothouse here at home. A lamb that has grazed in New Zealand might not use more resources than one raised on feed in Britain.

Perhaps you have a weakness for mangoes flown in from Kenya. Then you should eat mangoes. But add the carbon dioxide for transportation — about five times the weight of the fruit — to your personal greenhouse gas calculation. Choose four pounds of carrots instead of four pounds of tomatoes and you're back to even.

58.

SAVE A THREATENED SPECIES. Being a friend to wildlife isn't
only a matter of caring about photogenic species with cute
babies. In 2005 around 65 per cent of non-marine mammals and
birds and 22 per cent of fish, amphibians and reptiles assessed
were considered "threatened". Nearly a quarter of invertebrates
and around a third of seed plants and ferns are threatened
or nationally scarce. All this points to wider — undesirable
— environmental changes.

   You can help conservationists inventory species in your
area. For birdwatchers, the British Trust for Ornithology
promotes conservation through volunteer-based surveys. For
other wildlife sightings, see if there is a county recording
club or local records centre in you area. The National
Biodiversity Network is building a web-based databank that
consolidates reports from researchers and the public to
chart wildlife throughout Britain so that "wise and informed
decisions can be made to ensure our natural environment is
diverse, rich and sustainable".

59.

EAT A THREATENED SHEEP. Paradoxically, some species are
threatened because there is no market left for breeders.
Buying meat from a domesticated breed like the Herdwick Sheep
— beloved by one Mrs William Heelis, better known as children's
author Beatrix Potter — can also mean saving a unique landscape, as grazing has shaped the British countryside for
centuries.

60.

<u>GIVE TO THE POOR.</u> It requires a certain level of material well-being to be able to make positive environmental choices. Hundreds of millions of people still live in such poverty that a job in a polluting factory or on a plantation drenched in chemicals would be considered a blessing.

The fact is, you already give — when you pay taxes.

Nearly one-third of the poverty reduction projects supported by the Department for International Development include explicit environmental targets. DFID spending in 2005 on environmental improvements in Africa, Asia, Eastern Europe and Latin America amounted to some £576 million.

So keep helping the less fortunate improve the environment. Support the government's aid to developing countries at the same time you give to causes close to your heart.

61.

PLAN YOUR CITY. Building suburbs and shopping centres on prime agricultural land may make economic sense today, but that doesn't mean it won't be seen as madness tomorrow. The more our cities and towns sprawl out, the more energy we use.

Land use planning processes are open to public input. Look to see what the general plan calls for in your area, and pay attention to proposed building projects. Have your say before construction begins, while there's still time to make changes and explore alternatives.

The Earth's population is expected to be 9 billion souls by the year 2050. Let the UK be a model for building smart urban areas and saving our fields for growing food and biofuels.

62.

<u>FLY SMART.</u> Unfortunately, air travel uses a lot of energy. And green fuels for aeroplanes aren't here yet. To be sure, the newer planes are more efficient than the old ones, but that savings is more than balanced by overall growth in miles travelled.

Air traffic accounts for about 3 per cent of total carbon dioxide releases worldwide. Many scientists believe the global warming effects are greater because that carbon is released at high altitudes.

But the opportunity to leave behind Britain's winter damp for a sunny beach with a few hours in the air is just too enticing for many. And there's no need to give up on such luxuries if you make an attempt to balance your lifestyle with some fairly painless sacrifices elsewhere.

Don't drive more than you need to. Step up to a green car or ride a bike to work. Shop for what you need, not as a form of therapy. Then you can treat your family to that holiday in a warm, exotic locale. Just don't waste your "carbon quota" on other things that you can easily do without.

Like sitting still in traffic every day.

63.

ENMOY YOUR PLEASURE BOAT. Just don't let your marine behaviour add to pollution. Sailing or rowing is of course preferable to tearing up the water in a motorboat. If you do buy a motorboat, four-stroke engines are a better environmental choice than two-strokes, where almost a third of the fuel goes unburned into the water.

Look for an eco-label on any hull paint you use. Toxins from hull paint are released over time, especially during underwater hull cleaning. They may be absorbed by mussels and worms, and are then passed up the food chain to fish, birds and humans, posing health risks.

Carefully choose the products you use for bathing, dish-washing and laundry on or near the water. And always wait until you come to a harbour with proper sewage disposal before emptying your toilet tank.

64.

COMPARE ELECTRICITY CONSUMPTION. Appliances may look alike
and offer the same features, but differ a lot in the amount
of energy they use. Try to choose the ones that use less. A
plasma TV can pull twice as much current as an LCD in the same
size. And a few extra inches in size can mean a big increase in
electricity use.

65.

COMPARE MORE. Choose a computer with an eco-label. It
will emit a weaker magnetic field and contain little or no
brominated flame retardants and heavy metals.

   Ask questions when you're shopping, and press for good
answers. When manufacturers hear from their retail partners
that consumers are asking about environmental features, they
are spurred into taking action.

   Eco-labelled electronics generally include markings on
components to make disassembly and recycling more efficient.

66.

DRESS GREEN. Some outdoor wear is treated with fluorine-based chemicals to repel water while allowing moisture from your body to get out. That's a great feature, but there are alternatives to fluorine, which may impact the health of workers in the manufacturing chain.

If you already own this type of clothing, there's no reason to throw it out, but if you re-treat it, use a fluorine-free substance.

When you're shopping, look for ecological waterproofing. And natural materials like cotton, wool and leather often do the job just as well as synthetics. After a shipwreck in 1915, Sir Ernest Shackleton and the crew of the Endurance spent 17 months in Antarctica dressed in gabardine wool.

How long are you planning to be outdoors?

67.

AVOID DRY CLEANING. Despite the name, there's nothing "dry" about dry cleaning. Your clothes are immersed in a solvent, usually perchloroethylene — also known as PERC — which is associated with unpleasant effects on the nervous system ranging from dizziness, fatigue and headaches to muscular incoordination and unconsciousness. PERC also contributes to depletion of the ozone layer.

The best solution is of course to buy clothes that you can wash yourself. But some dry cleaners are beginning to use much more benign solvents, including liquid carbon dioxide — which doesn't contribute to global warming, since the carbon is removed from the air in the first place.

68.

SHARE A CAR. It won't necessarily mean that the total mileage you drive will be less, but that will probably be the case. It certainly requires less energy to manufacture and maintain one car instead of two. And it's less expensive as well. With the money you save, it might be possible to upgrade to a green car.

Carplus, a national charity promoting responsible car use, claims that 10 million seats go empty on British highways every day. Car clubs represent a form of short-term hire, while car sharing (also known as liftsharing or ridesharing) matches up car owners with passengers who usually make a contribution toward fuel costs.

Similarly, you might consider joint ownership of a sailboat or lawn mower with a friend or neighbour.

69.

SEND A LETTER TO YOUR LOCAL NEWSPAPER. Letters to the editor are among the most read pages of the newspapers. In addition to helping shape public opinion, you might encourage politicians to follow their best instincts and support effective policies. See if you can encourage incentives for expanding the number of petrol stations offering green fuels, perhaps through reduced taxes. Support your local council's recycling efforts, or construction of wind power plants, or something else close to your heart.

Next, go online and send the same letter to relevant blogs.

70.

BE A GOOD BUILDER. Natural materials are preferable to synthetics, which can cause environmental problems in manufacturing and may even be hazardous to occupants' health. Before you choose building materials, find out where they come from and how far they have been transported. Be especially careful about threatened tropical woods.

Use of chromated copper arsenate (CCA) to pressure-treat timber against fungi and insects is now restricted in the EU, though it is still available. CCA is unpleasant stuff for you, your kids and the environment. Alternatives are available. You may still find old railroad sleepers or telephone poles impregnated with creosote and be tempted to use this timber for outdoor projects. Don't.

71.

SAVE AT HOME. More than one-quarter of Britain's energy use is in dwellings, and more than half of that goes to space and water heating. That means there are big carbon savings to be found right where you live.

Start with loft insulation. Simply adding a layer of 10-inch (250mm) thick insulation will save a lot of energy and money.

Wall insulation is another very cost effective way of reducing heat loss. Un-insulated cavity walls lose more heat than any other part of your home and could be costing you an extra £200 a year in wasted energy. Insulating cavity walls involves drilling small holes and injecting foam, beads or blown wool. Although the work has to be carried out by a professional, costs are likely to be recovered within 3-5 years.

72.

BE HEALTHY. When you get right down to it, your health isn't only your own business. If you get sick you have to get treatment, and the health care industry consumes enormous resources. Minding your health frees up care for those who may need it more.

So watch what you eat, take walks every day — or bike, go to a gym, play tennis or squash. Whatever you do, don't smoke. Besides coating your lungs with carcinogenic tar, tobacco farming takes agricultural land that could be used to grow food or biofuel.

73.

RIDE A BICYCLE. Anytime it's possible. Let's say you have a five-mile commute to work. Cycling instead of driving will cut your carbon dioxide emissions by more than 600 kilos per year and save you about £500.

74.

LOOK FOR THE ECO-LABEL. Don't believe that a brand is better simply because it's marketed as "green" or "natural". Look at the list of ingredients in food products or the power consumption of an appliance and make your own judgment. And a claim by the manufacturer that the package is recyclable doesn't say anything about the contents.

Common eco-labels include The Mobius Loop, EU Flower, Organic, Seafood, The Fairtrade Wood products.

Also, look for warning labels. If a product is a danger to the skin and eyes, or if it's poisonous, think carefully about whether it's really necessary to have it in your home. If it's bad for you, it will probably be bad for the environment.

75.

COTTON IS GREAT, BUT ... Cotton has to be considered a good choice for your clothing.

But industrialised cotton farming has some serious environmental impacts from artificial irrigation and excessive use of pesticides.

Until the 1960s the Aral Sea was the world's fourth-largest lake. Then Soviet central planners diverted its main rivers to irrigate huge farms growing cotton for export, and the Aral began shrinking. At its worst, in the late 1990s, the Aral was down to just 25 per cent of its original surface area and salinity had increased more than fourfold, killing most native fish and plants. A restoration project is helping, but the situation for the Aral is still dire.

Look for organically farmed cotton clothing if you can find it.

76.

RELAX BY A FIRE. An open fireplace provides a cosy spot to curl up with a good book on a chilly winter day. But be aware that you might not be getting as much heat into the house as goes up the chimney.

You'll get the best thermal effect and least environmental impact if you burn split hardwood that has dried for a year or two outdoors under a rain shelter and a week or two indoors.

Never burn pressure-treated lumber, painted or glued wood, chipboard, plastic or rubbish, as these can produce fumes that are good neither for you nor your chimney.

A modern enclosed wood stove sacrifices some of the cosiness but puts much more of the firewood's heat energy into the room.

77.

BE COOL. Air conditioning can increase your car's fuel consumption by up to 10 per cent. On the other hand, driving with the windows down causes drag that burns more fuel. So perhaps the best rule of thumb is to open a window in town and use the A/C on the motorway.

Most cars with automatic climate control have a switch to manually turn off the A/C. But it's a good idea to turn it on once in a while to let the liquid coolant circulate. This keeps seals in the system from drying out and leaking.

Even when it's cold out some automatic climate controls will go on to reduce humidity.

78.

<u>PAINT PRETTY.</u> Paints can be of concern due to the toxic
chemicals they contain. Volatile Organic Compounds (VOC) are
the solvents and other chemicals in paint which evaporate
during use. These can damage the environment and affect
human health. You can help reduce the impact of paint on the
environment by choosing products with a low VOC level — try
B&Q who have designed a labelling system which states the VOC
content. Better yet, use water-based paints.

Some solvents in glues have also been found to be highly
toxic and pose a risk to the environment, wildlife and human
health. When purchasing strong adhesives, try to buy water-
based, solvent-free glues and keep them away from children
at all times.

79.

__CLEAN THE OLD-FASHIONED WAY.__ Many of the cleaning agents
for sale in your local supermarket contain harmful chemicals.
Chances are you don't need more than dishwashing soap and a
general-purpose cleaner.

  Try cleaning the way your grandmother did. Vinegar or lemon
juice work fine on the toilet and tiles. Vinegar removes stains
and dishwashing liquid cleans windows. Make your oven shine
again by painting the inside with a solution of simple liquid
soap and leaving it for an hour or so at low heat. Spills on
stuffed furniture can be attacked with baking powder in warm
water.

80.

CHANGE YOUR HAIRSTYLE. A test of 38 different gels, sprays and mousses uncovered a lot of bad news for health and the environment.

All the tested hair products contained chemicals known or believed to be allergenic, carcinogenic, mutagenic or disruptive to the hormonal and reproductive systems. The amounts used are so small that the danger is minimal, but chemical exposure is always a greater concern for young people. And who uses the most styling products?

81.

CHANGE YOUR MAKEUP. This isn't so easy. There are plenty of eco-labelled soaps, shampoos, conditioners and shower gels. But it's a lot harder to find green cosmetics.

At a minimum, try to simply choose products with fewer ingredients. If you find a cream with 27 different chemicals that you can't pronounce, chances are some of them will be things that you and the environment can do without.

82.

BUY CERTIFIED ORGANIC. An "organically grown" guarantee lets you know that you're bringing home healthier food. As the Soil Association says, "Put simply, organic food contains more of the good stuff we need — like vitamins and minerals — and less of the bad stuff that we don't — pesticides, additives and drugs."

A certified organic farm won't pollute lakes and rivers with pesticides that wind up on our plates when we eat fish. Certified banana plantations aren't sprayed against weeds, insects and fungi; conventional growers spray 40 to 50 kilos of various poisons every year.

An easy choice? Not always.

There's a strong case for the industry argument that artificial fertilisers and pesticides are essential to feeding the world's burgeoning population. Just look at the tripling in global grain production between 1950 and 2000, as land devoted to these crops grew by just 10 per cent. Organic farms generally produce less per acre, and if everyone ate organic we'd be forced to have much more land under the plough, limiting biodiversity and causing other environmental problems. But markets work, and demand for organic food leads to improved production methods and higher yields.

Organic farmers are commonly seen as fuzzy-headed dreamers. But perhaps it's worth putting at least some of your food budget into the hands of visionaries with an explicit ethical agenda, at the expense of the cold calculations of global agribusiness.

Easy or not, it's your choice.

83.

<u>STUDY CHEMISTRY.</u> There are more chemical compounds in the average home today than there were in the average laboratory a century ago. The flow of chemicals through our homes, work-places and natural surroundings is one of the most serious environmental threats we face. Cancer-causing PCB is found in fish; meat contains flame retardants; cheese has traces of plastic softeners; game is tainted with organic chlorine compounds from pesticides. The list goes on.

In December 2006 the European Parliament passed a law known as REACH, aimed at reducing public exposure to hazardous chemicals. While REACH brings some positive changes, espe-cially regarding information on chemical safety, many environmentalists see it as too weak.

Decisions made in Brussels and Strasbourg will continue to weigh heavily on the future of chemicals in European society. If you're concerned or just wondering, send an email or letter to your MEP.

And don't skip voting for the EU parliament, not least because it's the only EU institution directly answerable to voters. In 2004, only 38.8 per cent of eligible British voters cast ballots, lower even than the abysmal 45 per cent European average turnout. If chemical legislation was the only issue (and it certainly isn't) we'd have plenty of reason to do better.

84.

<u>CONSUME LESS.</u> All due respect for low energy lamps, eco-labels, A+ white goods and Fairtrade coffee, but we can all do more to lessen our personal impact on poor Mother Earth.

The first step is to recognise that you can't reduce carbon emissions by going shopping, even at the right stores.

A good second step is to simply use less. Certain clothes, cars and computers might use less resources than others, but more consumption always means more energy, natural resources and pollution.

Everything you buy causes carbon emissions in manufacturing and transportation, and usually during use and final disposal as well.

Since 1993, a group called Adbusters has celebrated the last Saturday in November as "Buy Nothing Day", and the organisers claim it's now observed in more than 55 countries. It's fair to question the value of symbolic campaigns like this, but just pick a day and try to go 24 hours without spending any money. For most of us that's not easy, and making the effort can be an eye-opener.

85.

FIX IT. "It's not worth sending back for repair." Heard that one before? Think twice the next time it comes up. We are individuals and families, not corporate machines forced to maximise profits to justify our existence. From a purely economic perspective, it may well not be worth £175 to repair a £200 gadget. But it might still be a wise environmental choice if the repair cuts out the energy and resources required to make a new one, and the old doesn't wind up on the rubbish mountain just yet.

For some people life is a competition to collect the most stuff. For others, personal satisfaction comes from leaving the world in slightly better shape than they found it. What kind are you?

Try to see the virtue in making old things work instead of constantly buying new.

86.

USE USED. Anytime you can re-use something instead of buying a new one, you've done a good deed for the environment. Flea markets and auctions are always good sources for bargains, and the Internet is unparalleled for matching up buyers and sellers without wasting time on fruitless trips in the car.

87.

SUPPORT WIND POWER. The UK wind industry has reached the "significant milestone" of having more than 2 gigawatts (GW) of operational generation capacity.

Still, despite having some of the best wind resources in Europe, the UK is a long way behind the world's leading nation on wind power. Germany has more than 20 GW of wind energy capacity, 10 times as much as Britain.

The government has set a target of 10 per cent of electricity to be generated from renewable sources (including wind, solar, hydropower and biomass) by 2010. That would be a fairly substantial increase over the 4.2 per cent contribution from renewables today. Wind power is currently the most cost effective renewable energy source in a position to help meet that goal.

While the political process moves forward, look into installing your own windmill to pump water for the garden or generate electricity for a summerhouse or outdoor lighting.

88.

<u>WORK SMART.</u> Small measures can add up to big improvements in your workplace. Switch to low-energy lamps. Make double-sided copies. Get your company to switch to green cars. Cut business travel with videoconferencing. Recycle printer ink cartridges. Use bike messengers or plan ahead so documents and samples can be sent by Royal Mail. Use recycled paper.

Go a step further and have your company perform a carbon audit, and then develop a concrete action plan for reducing greenhouse gas emissions.

Suggest that your IT department buy ecolabelled computers. Look around for appliances drawing electricity on stand-by. Computers, printers, coffee-makers and copiers should be turned off completely when not in use.

Whenever possible, distribute internal information in .pdf format instead of printed on paper.

Suggest a programme to certify your company or organization to the ISO 14001 environmental management standard.

89.

DO YOUR HOMEWORK. If it's hard to choose between driving the car and taking the bus to work, maybe you should just stay home. If you have an office job, see if it's possible to devote a day every now and then to do paperwork, make phone calls and perform other tasks that you can do from the kitchen table.

Keep in mind that half of all the emissions our planet has to absorb come from job-related travel.

90.

SIT LONGER. Check the materials that go into the seemingly priceworthy sofa or stuffed chair you're considering: amide plastic resin, nylon, polyester, polyether foam, polypropylene, epoxy powder-coated steel, chromed steel and viscose are all sources of considerable pollution in manufacture and disposal.

A more expensive model might have a completely different list on the declaration tag: beech or ash wood, saddle-girth, leather, hemp, linen, excelsior, horsehair and cotton wool are generally better environmental choices. And the higher-priced furniture will likely age much better and be a better buy in the long run.

91.

OBEY THE LAW. Our governments and civil services are home to many thoughtful, intelligent public servants who actually give a great deal of thought to their decisions. Politicians and bureaucrats at the EU, national, regional and local levels are (mostly) genuinely concerned and informed individuals working hard to protect the environment. Very few of our laws and regulations are created just to make your life more difficult.

To gain an understanding of how environmental threats are defined and addressed, read about the UK Government Sustainable Development Strategy. The plan encompasses a suite of 68 national sustainable development indicators falling into one or more of four priority areas:

- Sustainable consumption and production
- Climate change and energy
- Natural resources
- Sustainable communities

If you're concerned about a local issue, contact your council and find out who knows the facts.

The bureaucracies certainly don't always get it right, and grand plans often fall victim to inadequate funding, staffing or follow-through. But informed citizens making their views known can do a lot to break institutional inertia and get results.

The very nature of environmental regulation usually means inconvenience or higher costs for someone, somewhere. But the more we all feel that the burden is equally shared, the easier it is to do our part.

92.

VENTILATE. During the winter, you need to let air into the house every now and then. But do it in short bursts rather than leaving a window slightly open all day. The best way is to turn down the heat, then open two windows and fill the house with fresh, cool air for a few minutes.

93.

OBSERVE AND RESPECT. It's not just a cliché; you are indeed a part of nature. Don't just view the natural world through a window; don't let it be something you visit now and then. Take a trip to a national park or nature reserve. The next time you hear about development encroaching on the little remaining untouched open space left in the British Isles, you'll have a clear idea what's being lost. Take a stand against poorly planned growth so your children and grandchildren will also have the opportunity to experience open, unpopulated nature.

When you get out in the woods or along a desolate coast, think about how you fit in. Observe and appreciate. A quiet walk with a rucksack fills the senses far better than a motorised excursion.

94.

<u>DON'T LEAVE HOME WITHOUT YOUR MIND.</u> If you travel abroad, don't just go on autopilot. Check with a travel agent or look online for websites on ecotourism. The concept is as much about economics as ecology, because true ecotourism will ensure that the money you spend on holiday benefits local people.

Look for green certified hotels, which will meet basic standards for sewage disposal, water conservation, energy management and laundry procedures. Green hotels should also pay attention to the food served in restaurants and items sold in souvenir shops.

If you're planning a cruise, check to see if the ship runs on green fuel and is equipped with catalytic converters.

Put a little research into wildlife issues in the area you're planning to visit. The best protection for African gorillas, whales and other creatures is when there is more money to be made bringing tourists to see them than there is in shooting them, or developing their habitats.

Make sure you don't buy souvenirs made from skins of threatened species.

Travel thoughtfully. Don't take anything home that should be left where it is, and don't leave anything that doesn't belong.

95.

EAT VARIETY. That more than 80 percent of the world's spinach seed comes from Denmark may strike you as a banal factoid — especially if you hate spinach. But it's worth your interest, because it reveals the disturbing trend towards increasing monoculture, where the same species of plants are grown everywhere.

We need to strengthen biodiversity, where human activities support healthy ecological webs and landscape mosaics of agricultural land, lakes and streams, wetlands and forests. At the environmental summit meeting in Johannesburg in 2002, leaders of the world's governments adopted a UN convention calling for a reversal of biodiversity loss.

It's not enough to set aside reserves for threatened plant and animal species — and a spinach reservation would strike most of us as silly — but we can all help by "voting" for biodiversity with our food shopping choices. Look for different varieties of apples, tomatoes, lettuce and, yes, spinach.

96.

GET THE KIDS OUTSIDE. Build a treehouse, go camping, boating
and hiking, make a bird box, plant bushes for your local
butterflies, watch tadpoles turn into frogs in a pond in your
garden. Or just find a stump and make it your own outdoor
dining table. Get your family used to Sunday afternoons in the
woods with a packed lunch.

Try to find a nursery where the children are outdoors as
much as possible. Any time, any place; teach your kids that
nature is worth experiencing first-hand — and worth protecting
for the future.

97.

BE A ROLE MODEL. But don't overdo it. Avoid topics like "The energy required to produce all the world's dog and cat food ..." That will just turn off your pet-loving friends.

Instead, arm yourself with a collection of ohreallys. As in "Oh really? I didn't know that!"

• A single dripping tap can waste 25,000 litres of water in a year, or enough for 400 showers.

• An average tree can absorb 12 kilos of carbon dioxide in a year, and at the same time produce enough for a family of four.

• One person who pees in a lake for one day will add enough nitrogen to feed one kilo of algae.

• It takes 37 times as much energy to produce a kilo of chocolate as it does to produce a kilo of flour.

• Ten adults generate as much heat as a large radiator.

• A plastic bottle can remain in the ocean for 450 years.

• We are now using about 1,000 barrels of oil per second.

• A kiwi flown in from New Zealand causes carbon dioxide emissions of five times its own weight. If you eat a kiwi a day for a year, that's as much as a seat on a flight from London to Glasgow.

98.

USE LESS. Don't start your teeth-brushing routine by spitting out three-fourths of the toothpaste in the sink. Sure, it's insignificant (even if toothpaste costs more per pound than the better cuts of beef), but it helps to keep the right attitude. If the directions on the cleaning solution say to use a capful in a bucket of water, the floor won't get cleaner if you dump in a full cup. Your laundry won't get whiter from overdosing the detergent. Cut your living costs and save the planet at the same time.

When you cook, don't make so much you have to throw food away or let it grow mould in the back of the fridge. Instead, put out a fruit plate at the end of the meal so your family can eat a little more and a little healthier.

It all adds up to fewer resources for production, less energy for transportation and less waste to the landfill.

99.

TRANSPORT LESS. Look around you. How many of the things in your house were made locally? To be sure, it's far from easy to cut carbon dioxide by buying local. We don't make much in the way of consumer electronics in the UK, for instance.

Another problem is that it's meaningless to compare distances alone, since the goods we buy are brought to us by different means of transportation. Take wine as an example. One study shows that a properly loaded container ship releases one-sixth as much carbon dioxide per kilo as the most efficient lorries. So an environmentally aware Liverpudlian might have a cleaner conscience buying a nice red shipped from South Africa rather than trucked from Spain.

Another study says the difference is 13 times as much, so a ship from Australia would still beat the lorry from Spain.

But then along comes a third study showing that most shipping is inefficient, since many vessels still run on older diesel engines with no catalytic converters. In that case it's best to stick with the Spanish Rioja.

The truth is that it's almost impossible to know whether you're making the right choice from a transportation perspective. What is clear, however, is that it's worth supporting political leaders willing to take on powerful industries, for instance by insisting that the Kyoto agreement on climate change should include sea and air transport. They are currently exempted, which means there are neither carrots nor sticks to push them toward cleaning up. Including transport in the emerging carbon trading regime would be a step in letting market forces steer consumption habits toward better environmental solutions.

100.

<u>CALL A POLITICIAN — AGAIN.</u> Maker it clear that environmental issues make a difference in how you vote.

Such calls led councils in cities like Barcelona and Oxford to require solar heat in all new construction.

Such calls led the governor of California to promise to "show the world that economic growth and the environment can coexist."

Such calls led Britain's prime minister to call for a 60 per cent cut in carbon dioxide emissions by 2050.

Comments

Figures refer to the points in the main text.

6. European Commission's Carbon Calculator. www.mycarbonfootprint. eu/carboncalculator1_en.asp

9. Check out www.greenelectricity. org to see which alternatives are available where you live.

12. The Marine Stewardship Council's guide is available for download at www.fishonline.org/ information/MCSPocket_Good_Fish_ Guide.pdf

18. Organic wines are easy to find online. Try Sainsbury's (www. sainsburyswine.co.uk), the Sunday Times Wine Club (www.sundaytimes-wineclub.co.uk), and Virgin Wines (www.virginwines.com). About Organics (www.aboutorganics.co.uk).

19. You can find contact information for your MEP at www. europarl.europa.eu/members/public. do?language=en.

26. See www.fairtrade.org.uk.

28. Information about wormeries is available from www. originalorganics.co.uk/wormeries. htm.

30. Read more at the WFD Information Centre: www.euwfd.com.

39. The "Eat the Seasons" website (www.eattheseasons.co.uk) is an excellent guide to help you find the right food for the time of year.

40. The UN Food and Agriculture Organisation (FAO) has produced "Livestock's Long Shadow", an excellent report on the impacts of animal farming worldwide, from greenhouse gas emissions to deforestation and water pollution. See www.fao.org.

43. The United Nations Environment Programme (UNEP) has launched a worldwide tree-planting effort called the "Billion Tree Campaign". See how you can get involved at www.unep.org/ billiontreecampaign.

47. Locally sourced, sustainable charcoal can be bought from www. bioregional.com or www.graigfarm. co.uk.

48. Look for certificates issued by the Forest Stewardship Council (FSC) or the Programme for the Endorsement of Forest Certification schemes (PEFC).

49. Britain's Drinking Water Inspectorate (www.dwi.gov.uk)

52. Britain directly produces just 2.2 per cent of the world's carbon emissions. But in a study called "The Carbon 100", Henderson Global Investors shows that as much as 15 per cent of the world's emissions are produced by companies listed in London. See www.henderson.com.

53. In recent years a trend has

emerged in which environmental reporting is combined with declarations on how a company handles social and economic issues, for instance inspections to ensure that foreign suppliers respect trade union organising rights, don't employ child labour, and help local communities grow sustainably. Smart investors read these Corporate Social Responsibility (CSR) reports as part of the risk assessment process, and on the sound theory that effective environmental and social management is a sign of good corporate governance.

As a shareholder or consumer, you have every reason to look into the CSR practices of companies you own or patronise. Most CSR reports will contain a certain amount of "greenwash", spotlighting minor, anecdotal changes, and that's to be expected. But there should also be some element of genuine disclosure. Look for statements indicating that the company recognises a need for improvement in a certain area.

Does the report specify targets for the future? If the company brags that carbon dioxide emissions from its manufacturing plants have fallen over the last decade, look to see if it also stakes out goals for coming years. Companies willing to tell the world what they plan to achieve — and risk missing targets — are the ones working hardest to clean up.

56. The EU's environment website could be better organised, but it's still a good source for information about chemicals: www.ec.europa.eu/ environment/index_en.htm.

58. The British Trust for Ornithology (www.bto.org). The National Biodiversity Network (www.nbn.org.uk).

65. Greenpeace maintains an excellent "Guide to Greener Electronics" that ranks manufacturers on a range of issues, from chemicals and recycling to "global policies and practices" (www. greenpeace.org/international/ campaigns/toxics/electronics/how-the-companies-line-up).

68. Check out www.carplus.org.uk, where you can find links to car clubs and car sharing.

74. The "Mobius loop", three arrows turning back on one another to indicate that a product is recyclable or made from recycled content. When a "recycled content" claim is made, the label should indicate what percentage of the item is made from waste materials.

EU Flower: The EU's eco-label programme helps you make better environmental choices by analysing impacts from the entire lifecycle of a product and successively raising the bar for which ones qualify. ec.europa.eu/ environment/ecolabel/index_en.htm

Organic: There are a number of logos used for organic goods. There is some controversy over whether this confuses the British consumer or adds to choice. One of the best known is the Soil Association certified label. www. soilassociation.org/certification

Seafood: The Marine Stewardship Council's blue eco-label can be found on more than 300 seafood products in supermarkets, and MSC works closely with the UK food-service industry to encourage schools and restaurants to serve sustainable seafoods. www.msc.org/

The Fairtrade Mark is an independent consumer label which appears on products as an independent guarantee that disadvantaged producers in the developing world are getting a better deal.

Wood products: The Forest Stewardship Council (FSC) has developed a unique system of independent forest certification and product labelling, helping consumers identify timber and products from responsibly managed woodlands. www.soilassociation. org/forestry.

A complete list of eco-labels used in the UK is available from The Department for Environment, Food and Rural Affairs: www.defra. gov.uk/environment/consumerprod/ pdf/shoppers-guide.pdf

82. See www.soilassociation.org and www.organicconsumers.org.

83. See www.ec.europa.eu/ environment/chemicals/reach/reach_ intro.htm.

84. See www.buynothingday.co.uk.

87. A single wind generator can reduce greenhouse emissions by up to 20,000 tonnes, or as much as 7,000 cars produce in a year.

But there is furious debate across Britain over the impacts of building thousands of wind turbines, especially since they often must be sited in sensitive areas where strong winds consistently blow. Even environmental activists are divided.

Concerns about wind power include wildlife disruption, draining of peat bogs (from construction of foundations and access roads) and aesthetic pollution of majestic mountain peaks. Against those threats are greenhouse gas emissions, air pollution and security risks that accompany oil, coal and nuclear power generation.

Reasonable people can disagree. It's beyond reasonable doubt, however, that global warming is upon us, that human activities are causing it, and that the consequences could be devastating for the environment and for future economic well-being.

Yes, there are negative impacts from wind power, but the alternatives are considerably worse.

91. UK Government Sustainable Development Strategy (www. sustainable-development.gov.uk). DEFRA, the Department for Environment, Food and Rural Affairs, also maintains a comprehensive website covering a broad range of policy areas (www.defra. gov.uk).

94. The International Ecotourism Society (www.ecotourism.org) is a great resource for the environmentally aware traveller.

Production Facts

To produce this book with the least possible environmental impact, materials and business partners have been carefully selected.

Body printed on 150g Papyrus Multiart matte, manufactured by Stora Enso at the Grycksbo paper mill, which is certified according to ISO 14001.

Flyleaves printed on 150g Munken Lynx, which has received the Forest Stewardship Council eco-label; manufactured by Arctic Paper. The Munkedals paper mill is certified according to ISO 14000.

Cover paper is Scandia 2000 from VIDA Paper AB, Sweden. Adhesives are biodegradable and are classified as non-toxic according to EU regulations.

Printing inks are based on vegetable oils; manufactured by Hostmann-Steinbergs, certified according to ISO 14001.

Woven cloth binding, Calicut 328/043 Regatta from Schneidler Grafiska AB, is made from 100% cotton facing a 35g acid-free paper. Dyed with natural pigments.

Picture Sources

Figures refer to the points in the main text. All images from Johnér picture agency.

Front cover:
  Lena Granefelt
Back cover:
  Jeppe Wikström
1 Photonica
2/3/4 Mats Widén
5 Peter Ahlén
6 Susanna Blåvarg
7/8 Image Source
9 BrandX
10/11 Per Ranung
12 Hans Carlén
13/14 Jeppe Wikström
15 Per Ranung
16 Lena Granefelt
17/18 Karin Berglund/
  Naturbild
19 Per Ranung
20 Lars Thulin

21/22 Stefan Rosen-
  gren/Naturbild
23/24/25
  Mikael Dubois
26 Per Ranung
27/28 Per Ranung
29 Jeppe Wikström
30 Jeppe Wikström
31/32 Philip Laurell
33/34 Jeppe Wikström
35/36 Ulf Huett
  Nilsson
37/38 Image Source
39/40 Max Brouwers
41/42 Nicho Södling
43/44 Ewa Ahlin
45/46 Jeppe Wikström
47/48 Elliot Elliot
49/50 Per Ranung

51/52/53 Per Ranung
54/55 Mats Hallgren
56 Elliot Elliot/
  Etsabild
57 Per Ranung
58/59 Workbook
60 David H Wells/
  Photonica
61 Image Source
62 Magnus Rietz
63 Jeppe Wikström
64/65 Jeppe Wikström
66/67 Bengt Hedberg/
  Naturbild
68/69 Per Ranung
70/71 Elliot Elliot
72/73 Mats Widén
74/75 Per Ranung
76/77 Jeppe Wikström

78 Mats Hallgren
79 Per Ranung
80/81 L Ancheles
82 Mårten Adolfson
83 Per Ranung
84 Lars Thulin
85/86 Per Ranung
87 Image Source
88 L Ancheles
89/90 Jeppe Wikström
91 Jeppe Wikström
92/93 Per Ranung
94 Image Source
95 Per Magnus Persson
96 Susanne Walström
97 Stefan Wettainen
98 Jeppe Wikström
99 Jeppe Wikström
100 Alexander Crispin

This book has been published
with generous support from the following companies:
SEB Securitas AP Fastigheter

Advisory Board:
Georgia Destouni, Professor of Hydrology, Hydrogeology and Water Resources,
Stockholm University, Sweden
Professor Andy Gouldson, Director of the Sustainability Research Institute at
the University of Leeds
Lennart Möller, Professor of Health risks in the environment, Karolinska
Institutet, Stockholm, Sweden
Natalie Suckall, Teaching and research assistant, School of Earth and
Environment, University of Leeds
Anders Wörman, Professor of River Engineering, The Royal Institute of
Technology, Stockholm, Sweden